Testimonial Praises

Up for Grabs

Irma Jean Driver

Dorrance Publishing Co
585 Alpha Drive
Pittsburgh, PA 15238
Visit our website at *www.dorrancebookstore.com*

ISBN: 979-8-8868-3148-1
eISBN: 979-8-8868-3726-1

My Prayer

I pray this book awakens and the words are carefully taken.
That it touches the reader
Warms the heart of the believer
And brings awareness to the mind of a sinner to receive it.
In Jesus name. Amen

❧❦❧

Dedicated to my mom Annie Mae Gipson, who, at the age of 82, wrote a cookbook titled Mother Annie Mae Gipson's Kitchen Table. *Cooking was her passion. Her book was filled with so much love. It reminded me of my love for God and was a huge inspiration for me wanting to move forward with my book.*

She didn't get to see it come to fruition, but I still remember how she encouraged me and offered her support. I can visualize the smile on her face, her knowing that I followed in her footsteps.

Contents

A New Day

Today is another chance, another day to take a stance.

Another day to praise the Lord.

To let Him know of Him, you are a part.

Another day to help save a soul,

It doesn't matter, young or old.

Another day to renew the mind,

Only blessings you will find.

Another day to be a blessing,

Another day to learn a new lesson,

Another day to try and do good

Simply because you should.

Another day to lend a helping hand,

To help the fallen up and help them to stand.

Another day to speak of upheaval,

To tell somebody it's all just evil.

Another day to sing and give praises unto the King.

Another day to shout and run all about.

Another day to pray, another day to say,

"Lord, I thank you for today in every way."

A Thought to Ponder

Have you ever wondered why we don't win souls?

Is it because we're not bold, or maybe we're just too cold?

Maybe we never speak a word,

And there's just nothing to be heard.

Maybe we're not following God's command

And just not lending a helping hand

Cause we're living by our own plan.

Or maybe we just don't show love,

The kind that comes from God above.

Maybe we're all about self,

And God's Word just sits on a shelf.

Or maybe we read and just don't heed.

Or maybe we think it's a joke,

And we just don't care how we talk to folk.

But isn't it funny, when we're in need,

We think of God, indeed,

But we don't think enough of Him to even plant a seed.

A seed can come in many forms and causes no one harm;

It could on behalf of someone else,

Cause them to go on their knees and

Ask the Lord to help them please.

It pleases God and warms His heart,

Him knowing you are a part.

A Willing Vessel

Man was meant to be a tool,

One which God could use.

People, places, and things

Became a must,

and God, they did not choose.

They obviously forgot who made them from dust and gave them a

pulse.

Man curses God's name and often blames;

They feel no remorse cause they have no shame.

Man thinks the fame was meant for them;

Jesus died on the cross, but they don't remember Him.

They don't seem to care what Jesus had to bear;

They just don't remember, not even a glimmer.

They just let their souls be lost

Without ever remembering the cost.

At Any Cost

Sometimes we can be offensive,
And the cost of it can be expensive.
It can be where a story begins
Or where a story ends,
Mostly for our own glory,
Simply because we told somebody else's story.
It could also hurt;
Did I mention it's where the Devil lurks?
We just need to confess;
We're being indignant and stirring up mess
In the home, street, or church.
It's still where the Devil lurks.
It can point blame and cause so much pain,
Yet we have nothing to gain.
A soul, it can cause us to lose
Cause our righteous anger, we choose to use.
The Bible tells us to hold steadfast,
How to win souls, and how to help them last.
If God's Word, we would obey,
Then all of us would be okay.

Awakening

Sometimes people leave this Earth

Without recognizing who truly gave them birth.

They live their lives and never grow

Cause Jesus Christ they just didn't know.

They were busy all over town,

Then wondered why so many ups and downs;

They didn't even have time to thank the Lord.

But if they had tried, it wouldn't have been hard;

They just didn't believe,

So they never did heed

Or even try to sow a seed.

When you tried to talk to them,

They would shut you down

With a face full of frowns.

But if only they had been apart;

One day, God would have pierced their hearts.

And they got smart and decided to choose,

So they, too, wouldn't lose,

Cause when you leave this Earth, your soul will need a place to go.

Unless you choose the way, the truth, the Light, it'll be hell for sho.

Be a Giver

Have you ever wondered why some people try
And others just get by?
Cause they don't close their hands
To God's commands.
When they obey God and give,
It takes nothing away but helps them to live.
Don't take this as funny,
But God don't need your money;
He has more than He can hold.
Haven't you heard,
His streets are paved with gold?
Stop being selfish, and get on board;
He already knows who will give and who will hoard.
You're looking in a ditch while you can own a river;
All you need to do is be a cheerful giver.

Be Led

Let the Holy Spirit empower us;

He rules our hearts, and evil, He sorts.

Let Him walk with us and guide our steps;

Let Him talk with us,

And let hearing be our help.

When being beat down, let Him be used all over town.

 He teaches us: Evil, we don't have to accept it.

The Holy Spirit teaches us to be quiet.

Listen, and you'll find,

The Holy Spirit is designed

To work with your mind.

Boasting

God's timing is unlike ours:
We look at the clock, and off to the showers;
God can choose any hour
Simply because He holds the power.
He can take His time or make it happen;
We talk a good game but our lips are just flappin'.
Without Him, we would never wake up.
We would all just have an empty cup.
We go around bragging of what we can do on our own
Cause we say we are grown.
But God has been in control
Since the day we were born.
God is the Master; without Him, life is a disaster.
We need God in everything we do,
And that goes for both me and you.

But God

Sometimes when I'm at home

And I'm all alone,

I think about the throne,

And who sits on.

And what it must be like to hold all the power

Of every second, minute, and hour.

What it must be like to carry that load;

And just how much He's owed.

How He carries the weight of the world

Of every man, woman, boy, and girl.

My! how His hand must be big and strong

And how He holds us all and protect us from harm.

How He watches over us while we sleep

and how our souls, He keeps.

How He keeps His angels in flight,

And how our battles, He's ready to fight.

How He answers our prayers,

And how He provides for our affairs.

He has to love us all

To answer all these calls.

How great His love has to be

To put up with you and me!

I pray His face, one day,

We'll see.

Choices

Life is but a vapor, and then we are no longer here.

Things we take for granted,

Not always as they appear.

We waste our time on foolish things,

Like negative flings and false kings.

A relationship with God is worth so much more

Cause He holds the key that opens the door

To peace and joy, and happiness, too.

I would think about this if I were you.

I would do it today and not wait for tomorrow

Cause life so quickly could turn into a horror.

Life was never meant to make us bad or sad;

God meant it for good and to make us glad.

But by the choices we make,

Our own lives we take—

Not necessarily by a gun,

But depending on which race we run.

Salvation or Damnation.

Choose Love

Love should not be silent;
Love should be calm and serene.
Love should be heard;
Love should be seen.
Love should be kind and not mean.
Love is mandatory
For our daily lives, and love is
What's needed when Jesus arrives.
Through hate, condemnation;
Before God, royal—a conversation.
One will lead you over here; the other,
Over there.
One is a heavenly home;
The other is nowhere love is
Given unto us worldwide,
Yet we're unable to decide
That love comes from God,
Whom we should abide.

Confident

When I don't know what to do,

Lord, I call unto You.

I fall down on my knees, and I begin to pray;

Sometimes I'm lost for words and don't know what to say.

Lord, have mercy on me, please; put my mind at ease.

I know You hear me when I call

Cause You never let me fall.

Confrontation with the Mind

Mind, ole mind of mine,
How shall I confront thee?
Sober or with wine?
While one is clean and the other untwine,
I'm torn between a drink and my mind.
I can't rest cause my life is a mess;
What shall I do? Must I confess
To what I am—to the "I Am"?
Oh, Lord, I come to You with clothes worn and my mind torn,
Seeking You, oh, Lord, to be reborn,
Though they look at me with frowns,
Like their pity for me drowns.
Mind, ole mind of mine,
I now know how to confront thee
Cause the Great "I Am" has set me free.

D-R-U-G-S

(Devil Ruining Users' Good Souls)

<u>D</u>

<u>Decide, Dazzle, Declare:</u>

To make a change;

To overpower darkness with life;

To be open and honest about insanities.

<u>R</u>

<u>Rest, Resist, Result, Repent:</u>

You must start over;

You must fight against demons;

You must have regrets, feel remorse;

You must see it through to the end results.

<u>U</u>

<u>Usurp, Utmost:</u>

To take back by force everything the Devil stole from you,

Number one being sanity.

<u>G</u>

<u>Gratify God:</u>

Thank Him for His favor, for everything bestowed upon you,

For His sufficient grace and mercy.

(cont.)

<u>S</u>
<u>Sobriety, Sanity, Salvation:</u>
You must be sober;
You must be sensible;
You must be redeemed.

Dear God

Dear Father God,

I thank You for Your love;

It keeps me praying to You above.

Because it keeps me in perfect peace

And makes my whole life better,

I thought I'd take the time to write You this letter.

Just in case you never knew,

I love you, Lord, I really do.

For it's Your Son Jesus' name

That helps me to sustain.

Deep

We come to church and sit on the pew,

Waiting for God to make us new.

Without ever doing our part, we never give God praise;

Our hands, we never raise.

We never even stand for fear of man;

When we do, work and the sun fade.

At the end of the day, we want to get paid.

Tic-toc, we look at the clock;

We don't even take the time to speak to the flock.

We say we love God, but the way we show it is kinda odd;

We hold God in a bubble, only for when we are in trouble.

We hold out our hand to reach for a blessing;

We just continue to do it cause we never learn a lesson.

We bring nothing in;

We take nothing out,

Not even what the message was about.

God is looking for somebody real;

He's looking for souls to heal.

Do you really not believe, your heart, He can't feel?

Everyday Blessing

The number of breaths you take doesn't measure your life,
But whether you use them for purpose or strife.
For the way you give and the way you live;
For the memories you make every day you're awake.
For the way you show love,
and for the way you thank your Father above.
For every breath you take; they are all to be counted,
For God's goodness' sake.

Everything You Need

Trust God, love Him,
And let us believe together
That He can bring us all
Through our stormy weather.
Give Him the glory for your story,
And let Him know you're holy.
Seek Him in times of sickness;
He'll be on your case with the quickness.
Seek Him for all your needs;
He is fulfilling, indeed.
Seek Him when in trouble;
He'll take it away and clean up the rubble.
Seek Him when you're broke.
Prepare to be amazed—God is no joke.
Seek Him when afraid; just imagine yourself
Where Jesus laid.
He got up, and He got out.
All God had to do was give a shout.
Every second, every minute of every hour,
Remember, God holds all the Power.

Faith

My Lord's daily bread I partake:

Every day I awake,

I read His Word,

And I plant it in my heart cause then I know it's heard.

When I thank my Lord that I can't see,

I always thank all three—

The Father, the Son, and the Holy Spirit, too,

Then I ask my Lord,

What would I do if it had not been for You?

Before He starts me on my way,

I take the time to say,

"I love you, Lord,

And throughout my day,

I'll still take time to pray."

For Love's Sake

What's on the inside should show up on the outside;

It should show to whom and where love abides.

It should show kindness, and help others with blindness.

It should make no excuses;

If I could, I would.

It should provide blessings in the hood.

It should help a child without, for a while.

Remember, it goes in a file.

It should help the old, even if just a cold.

We could one day see our lives unfold.

It should represent our Father above;

Everything we do should be done in love.

 The Bible says, "Love hides a multitude of faults,"

So I'm asking the Lord to let love be in your thoughts.

Friend or Foe

A friend picks you up when they see you falling down;
An enemy talks about you all over town.
A friend will show you love;
An enemy will walk by you and give you a shove.
A friend will give you food to eat;
An enemy will let you starve to defeat.
A friend will hold your hand;
You, an enemy can't stand.
A friend will be kind;
An enemy will try and steal your mind.
A friend is hard to find;
An enemy, well, it's how he dine.

Get Up

We fall down,
But if you can look up,
You can get up
And claim all the things that fill your cup.
Like peace, joy, faith, and hope;
All things needed to help you cope,
Using them throughout the day,
Helping to guide you on your way.
Peace is serene;
So much joy it brings.
Faith opens the door
For God to give you more.
Hope is a need
In order to succeed.
Because you're made in the image of God,
Getting up shouldn't be hard.
Pity parties, you try to throw,
But sometimes you just can't make the tears flow
Cause pity is a hinder
That contributes nothing to a mender.
On a daily basis, God fills your cup;
Remember, there's always something in it
To help you get back up.

God Forbid

God takes us from glory to glory.
He rewrites our story
Over and over,
The beginning and the end,
And all of them entail sin.
Experiences or interferences,
What difference does it make?
Cause either one, the Devil tries to take.
God needs some people He can use
To help spread the Good News.
To qualify, you don't need a chip
Cause whom he chooses, he equips.
On this journey, you'll need to work
To cover the places where the Devil lurks.
You'll need a watchful eye
Cause he's ready and willing to defy.
The Devil comes to steal, kill, and destroy;
You'll need to stay prayed up
To keep up with his ploy.
Compared to God, his power is weak;
On a daily basis, God's power, you'll need to seek.
Then while your story is being rewritten,
The Devil is being forbidden.

God's Masterpiece

Our children are a gift:
We should hold them in our hearts,
And we should give them a lift.
Us, sometimes, they bug.
We should still take them in our arms and give them a hug.
We should lead and guide them until they get grown,
Then we should allow them to be on their own.
And as they grow,
They should come to know
Because they've been told
Before they grew old
Whom they should lean and depend on,
And of course, He is the man on the throne.
They should carry Him wherever they go
Cause it helps to determine how their life will flow.
We pray for them and ask God to bless them
Cause we already know we can depend on Him.

Grateful

Lord, You guide me through my day
In every amazing way.
You keep my mind intact;
It's You who determines how I act.
I try to follow Your lead;
Your Word, I try to heed.
You give me food to eat;
You put shoes on my feet.
You put a roof over my head;
You protect me when I should be dead.
Thank you, Lord, for loving little ole me.
Thank you, Lord, for dying on the tree.
I count my blessings,
One by One.
Everything I need is already done.

Hatred – Deceit – Defeat

If the Lord didn't exist, what would you do?

When I thought about it, I thought about you,

So I compiled a list, just to name a few:

There would be no love; no Heaven above.

None would meet the mark

Cause the world would be so dark.

There would be no light; our only hope would be a fight.

Bats, knives, and guns,

To us, would be fun.

There would be no God;

No place to abide.

Sin everywhere, cause who would be there to care?

Children just as lost

With no one who could share.

Men and women living in shacks,

Many on their backs.

No morals—no values—no tomorrow;

Just living in horror.

Come, go with me to a better place.

If I were you, I'd make haste.

There is a home on high

That lives up in the sky,

But you can't just get by.

You don't have to be lost;

(cont.)

Pick up your cross.
Go as far as you can
Until you meet a man.
He'll show you the way,
But you must obey.
You just keep doing your best.
Let go; let God. He'll do the rest.

Help, Lord

Lord, I write this to stress, this world is in a mess.
You didn't intend it to be,
But what they don't know is only You can set it free.
If on a glass a picture of You, they painted
For all the things in this world, tainted,
And their minds were a mirror that they looked into,
Then when they looked, they'd only see You.
They could pick up all the pieces, and all the mess ceases.
They could see freedom land cause it's all in your hand,
Free from so many things You never intended to be;
And if again, they could believe,
There is so much more they could achieve.

His Grace

God's grace, we don't have to chase;
It's free to you and me.
His mercy endures as we mature.
His love, we'll eventually see.
He is who He proclaims to be.
His goodness is still up to date.
He's just downright great.
He's waiting for us to come through.
Our lives, He wants to make new.
We've heard the facts;
It's up to us to act.
If you're living on fate, then why wait?

A Hunger for God

Prayer is the key that gets you where you want to be.

If at first you don't succeed, pray:

Try falling down on your knees.

If again, you don't succeed, stay:

Pray until something happens.

Ask God to cast out your sin;

Tell Him how your life unfolds

And that you're told the answers He holds;

That Jesus Christ, you receive; the cross, you believe.

Ask Him to save your soul and make you whole.

I Believe

When God made us, He did it with dust.
He did it with a smile as He took us from the pile.
He gave us all sense with a head to think,
So we wouldn't need to depend on a shrink.
An ear to hear, and eyes to make a tear,
A nose to smell,
Arms and legs to help us up in case we fell,
A mouth to talk, to tell people about Him.
He gave us feet to walk and take it to them;
To tell a dying world that He is real.
To speak to our hearts,
Peace be still.

I Love You

Some people say what they say, and they do what they do,
But they never take the time to say, "I love you."
Maybe it seems like it's hard to say;
Maybe they could if they try to find a way.
Maybe it seems like nobody cares,
But it doesn't take away the hurt someone bears.
They smile and go on cause they would not dare
To say to you they think it's unfair.
If you feel this way and you know it's true,
Don't you be afraid to say, "I love you."

If Loving God Is Wrong, I Don't Want to Be Right

Because we're incomplete,

With God, we shouldn't compete.

He is the head and not the tail;

Unto Him, we should hail!

After all, He is well known.

The fame belonged to Him before we were born.

The world and everything in it, He created

For His benefit,

In His house, His many mansions;

It's not like He needs us to make any expansions.

Weapons formed against us,

He doesn't let prosper.

He arms us with the Gospel.

Some accept; others deny.

The question in my mind is, "Why?"

He preps us, just as He did from dust.

For us, loving Him should be a must.

The offering up of His Son

Wasn't done for fun.

He did it because all of us

Were, and still are, a work undone.

He meets our needs without ever getting up;

Right from the throne, He fills our cups.

He's got workers like me and you;

(cont.)

He instructs them on what to do.
At the bat of an eye, one flew by.
Now we've been made whole—
Thank God for saving our souls.

Image of God

Disaster is a terrible thing;
So much sadness, it brings.
Don't you dare think it can't happen to you;
It'll come without a clue.
One day, just when you think it's okay,
Out of nowhere comes despair.
You're not picked out to be picked on;
To sob, sigh, or moan.
The truth of the matter is,
Despair fell on the throne.
God gave His only Begotten Son
To smother out the fire that burns;
To save the souls of His people
As the world turns.
How awesome is He to care so much for you and me,
To set our minds free
From bondage of things gone wrong
And to think upon the cross
Where Jesus hung
To help us cope from disaster
And to thank Him for being our Master.

In God's Presence

God's presence, His Power can shift the atmosphere.

It can draw o' so near.

His love, you just want to hold so dear.

His mercy, His grace, encourages this race.

You can even do it at your own pace.

Don't be slacking; you keep going.

Count everything you do as a seed you're sowing.

When in His presence, you seek His face.

Be prepared to be amazed;

This is not a phase or a craze.

Pay attention to your life and watch your ways.

Invitation

God's presence is with us everywhere we go.
Show Him to the world, so they may know.
Whether a beautiful flower or a rain shower,
Show them who holds all the power.
Let them know His name carries a lot of weight,
And if they're dirty, He'll even clean their slate.
He'll turn their nights into day;
He'll lead and guide them and show them the way.
If they're sick and tired of going astray,
They just need to stop and take the time to pray:

"Lord, the Cross, I believe.
I am ready to receive;
Come into my heart,
Make me a part.
Lord, set me free;
It's in Jesus' name to whom I plea.
– Amen."

It's Hard but Fair

The Lord give, and the Lord take;
But what we need to realize, it is the Lord who make.
He has a plan He offers to all;
All you have to do is make the call.

The Call
"Lord, I'm tired, ready to change my life,
Ready to give up the mess and all the strife."

What He does for one, He'll do for another;
He doesn't like one and dislike the other.
He pardons our sins: children, women, and men.
He gives us blessings every day.
What's not of Him, He takes away.
He cleans us up and makes us shine;
No greater love, you'll ever find.
He is the Rock of Ages—
Just open His book and turn the pages.
There, you'll find everything you need.
But it's up to you to take heed.

Jealousy

Jealousy, it's like a disease

We seem to develop with all ease.

The symptoms can be many;

I wonder if we have any…?

It <u>spreads</u> at a <u>rapid</u> pace.

It's hard to <u>hide</u> when it's on your face

It <u>kills</u> the spirit, the one that's right;

It makes you <u>angry</u> and wanna <u>fight</u>.

It resembles a <u>thief</u>

Cause it <u>takes</u> away your belief.

It <u>tears</u> you up inside

And causes you to <u>forget</u> in whom you abide.

But there is a cure made up of all things pure:

He is the Lord; He is the King.

He is who defeats what the enemy brings.

It's all our jobs to watch and pray,

To stop the enemy from taking away.

The Lord assigns us work in all different areas,

So the world can see different scenarios

Cause one day, they may get on board,

And the work, we shouldn't hoard.

The kingdom of God is big and wide,

And we say we're on his side,

So let's ask the Lord to let us be free from jealousy.

Jesus Said

If ever you get a feeling that your life needs a healing
But you don't know what to do,
Just call on Jesus, and He'll see you through.
He'll wipe away your tears
And calm all your fears.
Let go, and give it to Him,
Then before your eyes,
It will all grow dim.
He'll bring you out of darkness
And lead you to the light.
The fight, you know you've won,
Cause your life will shine so bright.
Thank God.

Just Look

I look up, I look down;

I look all around.

I search for mankind, but it can't be found.

Have we thrown it all away

Or let it go astray?

For what, I can't tell.

But if we don't take it back, its heading straight to hell.

Jesus fell, but He got back up

Do we not drink from the same cup?

We hurt each other and kill each other, too,

While God is speaking to our hearts, "I love you."

Lest We Change

Doom and gloom,

That's news—

A worthy cause we are unable to choose.

Why are we so mixed up

While Jesus fills our cup?

Why do we rob, steal, cheat, and lie?

For it makes our Savior cry.

Whenever we need Him, He is always standing by.

Friends, family, foe,

Can knock on his door.

He'll probably answer and say,

"Why don't you love me more?"

We're only here for a while

Let's try to make our Savior smile.

At His return, we'll be so glad

We did not make our Savior mad.

Let Go, Let God

God can change your life and turn it around,
If only you let Him.
He can make it more abound.
He can turn bad to good;
If you'd let Him, He would.
He can bless you more than you know,
If through His Son, you let Him show.
He can give you hope, joy, and peace;
His love for you will never cease.

Links

Life is like a spinning wheel;

The names on it are sealed.

When God spins it and it stops,

Somebody's name is swapped.

I've come to the conclusion

That hell is not an illusion;

That I choose this day

To serve the Lord well,

So that my soul won't burn in Hell.

My sins were nailed to the cross,

So my soul wouldn't be lost.

Now it's owed to my Savior,

The One who paid the cost.

Because He's been and is good to me,

I owe Him so much; words can't express

What it's like to feel His touch.

I tell Him every day,

If He lets me stay,

I'll hold Him in my heart so dear

And always keep Him near.

I'll carry Him wherever I go

Just to let Him show,

And I'll tell the world,

A love like this

I've never known before.

Live or Die

Life gives you a reason why
While death takes away.
Life gives you choices
While death has no voices.
Life has history
While death is a mystery.
Life is a blessing
While death learns no lesson.
Life is all about making
While death is all about taking.
Life is love from God above.
Life learns;
Unlearned, death burns.

Look Again

What we want sometimes seems so far away,

But we continue to live day by day.

We wait and wait until we get tired,

And just when we think our time has expired,

We turn and walk away and there it is standing at the gate.

So we begin to pray:

"Dear Lord, I thank You, for I've been so alone,"

And He replies to us, "I've been sitting right here on the throne."

Lost and Found

Free your mind and let the rest follow,

No matter how deep or how hollow.

You follow your feet;

You dance to the beat.

You feed your mouth food to eat,

But the Savior, you don't try to meet.

You eat His food without giving Him thanks;

You don't even care. You just fill your tanks.

Life has an order, and it continually gets shorter.

You can't push God aside

No matter how you try.

He can take away his blessings and cause you to die.

You need to set aside a time for your mind to untwine.

Search your heart give everything to God

So that you and Him are no longer apart.

Try believing in Him

If your light been shining dim.

You trust God with all your might,

And watch Him turn up your light.

Lost

Every generation is weaker and wiser;

Somehow, they grow up as misers.

They seem to beg and borrow

Like there is no tomorrow

And cause others to be filled horror.

No hope. Nothing to help them cope.

What happened to our youth today

That they seem to be going astray?

Are we not leading the way

Or just afraid to say,

"Child of mine, if you don't wake up, here's what you'll find"?

A cell, hell, and not a voice to tell.

Our children today seem so caught up in a world of confusion;

Everything to them seems like an illusion.

The wiles of the Devil are real

And come to do nothing but steal, kill, and destroy

Whether girl or boy.

The streets are nothing but a trap

Filled with troubles and mishaps.

But the church is known as common ground,

Known as where the truth is found,

Known as where lives are turned around,

Known as where life is made more abound.

It is the way, the truth, the Light;

All found in Jesus Christ.

Love Thy Neighbor

Let us be spirit led and love thy neighbor as the Lord said.

Neighbors come and neighbors go,

But to a neighbor, we should open our doors.

Maybe they don't know the way they should go,

But we wear a glow, and we should let it show;

We should lend a hand if it will help them stand.

Maybe man can't, but God and us can.

We should be a vessel God can use

And share with our neighbors the good news.

We should tell them about Jesus and how He died

And why His Father is glorified.

Love thy neighbor, and let's all get along

Cause life is short and then we're gone.

Love

Love is just a four-letter word,

But love is never too often heard.

Love can hurt;

Love can heal.

Love is something that we can feel.

Love is kind and not hard to find.

Love is beautiful;

Love is dutiful.

Love is free for you and me.

Love is pure as a dove

Cause love comes from our Father above.

Main Line

The more the world turns,
The more we have concerns
Of all the upheavals caused by evil.
The Word is our tool, yet we let the Devil rule
Our minds, bodies, and souls
Until, right before our eyes, our lives unfold.
Our dreams, our goals…we lose them all.
That's usually when we make a call:
"Father, help us to withstand;
We put it all in Your hands.
We give You glory and the fame
It's in Your Son Jesus' name.

My Lord

When I go to bed at night,
I always hug You tight.
I lay my head upon Your chest
Cause then I know I'll rest.
I sing to You a melody
For who You are to me,
Then I fall asleep,
And in a dream, I peep.
I see so many blessings
From all Your lessons
When You wake me in the morning
And my pillow is soaking wet,
Cause in my dream You've shown me,
I ain't seen nothing yet.

No Respect of Persons

I thank You, Lord, for who You are;
Thank you for seeing enough good in me
To make me a star.
Oh, how I shine bright
To show others light;
To show them You
And be a witness You're true;
To tell somebody how You picked me up from the pits of hell,
How You healed my soul and made me well.
You did it for me; You can do it for them.
They, too, can be a star in your Heavenly realm.

No Stone Unturned

If we would stop and do some gazing,

Then we would find, God is amazing;

That as the Creator, concerning all things of beauty,

God did His duty.

No stones did He leave unturned,

Just as our souls, He didn't leave to burn.

Everything done for our benefit,

God did it.

He made a way for our sins to pay,

And a way of escape from hell one day.

Jesus died to set us free.

How sweet of Him to just let it be!

The love of God can be hard to digest,

But the proof is,

He gave us His best.

We thank You, God, for being You,

And for Your Son You gave, too,

Cause you gave up the Ghost;

It's Your amazing love we honor the most.

Our Families and Friends

We long to see our families and friends
Give their life to Christ
Cause condemnation won't be nothing nice.
Without ever having been groomed,
For the rest of your life, you'll be doomed
Cause you lived it in strife.
Unless God takes it away,
On that day, you'll have nothing to say.
Many of us have already missed the mark;
Today, you don't have to keep living in the dark.
The way has been paved to get your souls saved
If you'll just open up your heart
And ask God to make you a part.
He'll hear your prayer, and He'll answer you, too.
Your life, He'll make brand new.
However long it takes, the choice is yours to make;
It's strictly up to you to choose
Whether you win or lose.

Our Provider

Our Lord, we should obey,

For it is He who gives us another day

And starts us on our way,

Who gives us daily bread as we arise from our bed,

Who leads and guides us through the day,

Who gives us jobs and gives us pay,

Who gives us what we need, and

Only asks in return, His Word, we heed.

Out of the Box

I wish I was an eagle,
So I would have some wings.
Then I could fly to heaven to visit the King.
I could tell Him some things happening down here,
But He already knows cause to Him its oh-so clear.
But He can fix the problem, far and near.
I would tell Him thanks for all He's done,
Then we could share some laughter and just have fun.
Since we already have a fling,
Maybe I could take him a ring
Since He is the King.
But jewels and gems, He doesn't need;
This I know, indeed.
I would give it to Him anyway and just call it a seed.
I would throw my arms around Him and give Him a hug.
Maybe while I was up there, I would give y'all a plug.
I always wanted to touch the sky without really knowing why,
But now I know it's where we go
In this sweet bye and bye.

Praise

Thank You, Father God,
For this day.
Thank You, Jesus,
For all You had to pay
Thank You, Holy Spirit,
For guiding the way.
Just to thank all three
In one,
The Father—the Spirit—the Son,
Thank You, Lord, for blessing me
And taking my sins away.
Thank You, Lord, would seem
I was dead,
But You just keep on blessing me instead.
Lord, I thank You for who you are
And for keeping me when
I'm not up to par.
I thank You, Lord, that when I mess up,
You don't refuse to fill my cup.
I thank You, Lord, for all You're giving
And for the help You provide
For my daily living.
I thank You, Lord,
It's not all a dream;

(cont.)

That You truly are
Who You seem: good,
Great, amazing, and awesome, too.
Lord, what would I do
If it wasn't for You?

Ready or Not

If the world came to an end, where would you go?

Would you go to a friend or a neighbor's door?

But it's really not like that.

When Jesus returns, He's not coming for a chat;

He's coming with a command, and hopefully to take your hand.

Will you have your ticket in your hand, or will you just need a fan?

Will your soul go to heaven,

Or will it just burn when Jesus returns?

If I were you, I'd think about it;

It's truly worth concern.

You say, "I'll wait and maybe do it later,"

But life every day is a fader.

I know you think it doesn't matter,

But truly, one day, you'll have no data.

You say, "I'm not trippin,"

But in hell, that hot seat, you'll be grippin.

In heaven, you can walk around all day

And listen to musical instruments play.

You can watch the angels flutter by

In that beautiful sky.

No more pain; nothing but gain.

No more darkness; nothing but light.

But only if you get your soul right.

Real

Lord, search my heart.
May it reveal
If from You I'm ever a part;
If I'm living a lie and just getting by;
Or if it's real, and my heart, You can feel.
Lord, in my heart, a praise You should hear,
For the love of You, I hold so dear.
You should find a place where I've hidden Your Word
To help me run this race,
For I have built a nest,
A place for You to rest.
Lord, I believe You'll find
That I'm on Your side.
For it is in You, oh, Lord,
I will continue to abide.

Relationships

Some have many, and others, not any,
But a relationship is a beautiful thing,
Especially one with the King.
Some last, and others end,
And some just never begin.
Whether it starts with a smile
Or starts with a grin,
However it starts, you win.
Without it, you wouldn't even know the King
Or the wonderous joy He brings.
Singing, shouting, and praying all day;
Without a relationship, none of it pays.
A relationship is an entry
That's been around for centuries.
Use or lose,
What really matters is the ones you choose.

Respect Respects

Respect is humanistic
Of our characteristics,
Most of us born and raised
To expect respect.
It's relevant to honor, consideration,
And many other things;
It's truly a representative of our King
It can be given, earned, or shown,
Just as our Father does from the throne.
It's much needed in the world today;
Somehow, it seems, it doesn't have a leader
Cause it's gone astray.
In everything we do, respect plays a part.
In fact, respect is a matter of the heart.
It is give and take, not "do as I say."
Cause I make
Respect comes from a great place,
And respect is needed to run this human race.

Royalty

I'm made in the image of God;

As for me, God, I applaud.

I may have some things wrong with me,

But I'm made the way God wanted me to be.

He gave you yours, and He gave me mine

You think what you wanna, but I think I'm fine.

And not only am I dutiful,

I think I'm beautiful.

Because I'm so wonderfully made,

The beauty I exude will never fade.

Cause beauty is not what the eyes can see;

It's what's on the inside of thee.

My Father is rich, indeed,

And as His child, I have what I need.

His Word, I can rely on, and by now, you should know;

My Father sits on the throne.

Seek

God's presence is that of essence.

It causes my heart to leap.

His nature is that of which I want to keep.

His love so pure,

Intended to be dear.

His Word like wine,

The mind it confines.

His grace sufficient,

His mercy endures

In case you didn't know, your heart, it lures.

When you let Him in, He removes your sin:

Your old life comes to an end;

A new life begins.

With God on your side, you win.

Shameful Guilt

So many aches and pains Our Savior had to bear

Compared to all the darkness we shared.

Mostly caused by self,

Unwilling to hear cause, our ears were deaf;

Whenever a word come forth to heed,

We just catered to our own needs.

Just to help you, I'll name a few:

By alcohol and drugs and sweeping our mess under the rug;

By lying, cheating, and stealing;

Fooling ourselves, thinking we are wheeling and dealing;

By coveting our neighbors husband or wife,

Just living an adulterous life;

By indulging in inhuman acts,

Keeping secrets and calling them a pact.

Though love hides a multitude of faults,

 And by man, we didn't get caught,

We wrestled and wrestled until we got tired,

And then, to foolish things, we died.

Cause we accepted the truth

That from God, we could not hide,

So we cried out,

"Father, I surrender, I give up the hinder

I'm sorry for what I have done,

And I truly accept Your Son."

(cont.)

Then the Father replied,
"The way, the truth, the life,
Is all found in Jesus Christ."

Sin by Bite

Sin began with Adam and Eve;

God's Word, they didn't receive.

They thought what they did was okay,

But now we all have to pay.

When we heed God's Word and obey,

It gives us a chance to enjoy another day.

Nothing we do is done of our own;

It all comes from the Man on the throne.

Some people choose to believe it was Adam and Steve,

But there is sin in that, if you believe.

God created us to be like Him and not like them.

God gave us a plan to live by.

It didn't include guy to guy;

It didn't include girl to girl;

It proves we live in a messed-up world.

Of course, God would get the Glory,

But He can turn it around and change your story.

Sin can take you so far out and cause so much doubt.

But God, He'll give you hope and help you to cope.

Your life will never be the same

Cause now you trust His name.

Now you can see how all these things started from a bite

Cause they did what they wanted to, in their own delight.

So It Seems

Most children today are on their way to a burning hell,
Lest we teach them well.
Values, they have none; nothing on the inside.
They were never taught
To whom they shall abide.
They come up mad, sad, or bad,
Most of them raised without a dad.
Boys wear their pants down all over town;
Young girls in grown men's faces
Cause they don't know their places.
Mothers mostly with their girls,
Partying with them and slinging curls.
If we took them in our arms and loved them like we should,
Maybe some of the things we ask of them, they would.
We talk about them and beat them down, too,
Then when they look at us, they say, "We look like you."
If we ask the Lord to intervene,
then maybe it wouldn't look like it seems.
We need to stand for truth and help save our youth.

Spirits

Don't mess around and be used
Cause you got your spirits confused:
One holy; the other deceiving...
Be clear about what you're believing.
Holy is the name of God; the Father of
Deceit is the one that's odd.
Where he hangs his hat, he calls
It home. Now you imagine that.
Ever since he was kicked off the
Throne, he's continued to do
Wrong—nothing but evil upheaval.
He became a disaster to the
Master and started to hold
A grudge;
He had to give up his
Angelship, and he had to
Trudge, cause unlike him,
The power belongs to the King.
He lost his power, and he no
Longer has wings.

Tell Somebody

Have you told somebody about the goodness of God?

He knows all about us.

Do you think that's odd?

He knows what we do and when we do it, too.

Should that not be a clue?

He holds us in the palm of His hands;

He carries us as He makes footprints in the sand.

You ought to tell somebody about the goodness of God,

How He saved your soul

And made you whole;

How He opened doors that man can't close.

If you never told somebody He's good

And you tried Him for yourself, you would.

Thank You, Lord

Thank You, Lord, for Your glory,

For giving us a story

To tell and share

With some lost soul

Who did not know you care;

To help them not give up

Cause they drink from a bitter cup;

To help them with what they're going through

And to introduce them to You.

The Answer

When the Lord calls those who have fallen,
Instead of trying to heal, you just stand still.
How can He fill your cup
If you won't try to get up?
Just no hope to cope.
When he pushes you to the edge of your seat,
Somehow, along the way, Satan you meet,
Who comes to lie and defy
And comes to beat and cheat
And keep you falling off your feet.
When you stand up and claim your power,
It's like you're giving God a flower.
This must make God's heart expand
And make Him want to hold your hand.
Being just one of the many
Causes God to give you plenty.
The way we speak and the way we act
To others should have a great impact.
If one could win one,
There would be two.
But it all starts with me and you.

The Comforter

Lord, when I'm lonely,
I call on You only.
You hold me in Your loving arms
And free my mind from harm.
I call You any hour
Cause I know who holds the power.
I cast my cares upon You;
You always see me through.
I thank You, Lord,
For being tried and true.

The Goodness of God

It takes all kinds of people to make up the world—
Big or small, short or tall.
In need of something to do, how great would it be, Lord
If they all worked for You?
If they preached and teached
And your people, they reached;
If they sang and danced to You all day,
So You'd know they've come to live Your way.
You'd pour down blessings they couldn't hold;
They could call them fruit and put them in a bowl.
Every day, they could pick one
And give You thanks for what You've done.

The Great I Am

God is our all—
Father, Healer, Deliver, Forgiver.
He'll rescue you whether on dry land
Or up a river.
He'll show up day or night;
He's always ready for a fight.
Your battles, He can't lose;
He can win whenever He chooses.
If you never try Him, you'll never know.
He's just waiting for a knock on the door.
He already has your name on a cup;
He's just wishing He could fill it up.
Time is of essence and waits for no one.
God will still be sitting on the throne,
But before you know it, you could be gone.

The Order

Our first love is our Father above,
Then our family, too.
And to our friends, "We love you."
The Bible says, "Love thy enemies."
Hatred we must seize;
Man, we should not appease.
It's our Father we should please.
Satan's place is under our feet
Cause Jesus Christ,
He'll never beat.

The Pearly Gates

God is good, God is great;

It should be our goal to meet Him at the gate.

We need to meet Him in love—

We can't enter and hate.

It's gonna all be determined

By our faith.

We have two choices:

Paradise or hell.

Be careful how we choose.

With one we win,

But with the other, we lose.

God, we wanna uplift,

Therefore, we should take Him a gift.

In case we haven't heard, He loves hearing His Word.

One day, we'll come face to face

On how we ran this race.

We need to hide Him in our heart,

So we don't hear the word "depart."

The Power of God

He made the birds, the bees,

The trees, and the water in the seas.

During the day, He give us sunlight,

And at night, the moon shines bright.

The stars come out to play.

God, we just want to thank You

For giving us this day.

And when it rains, sometimes a beautiful rainbow,

He'll let show.

Through the clouds, we wish we could flow.

And when it storms, He sends a flash of lightning,

Taking us from darkness,

Bringing us to brightness.

He sends a roar of thunder;

Just like a cat, we're looking for something to get under.

God's will be done; we don't take it lightly,

And we don't take it for fun.

It's You, oh, Lord, choosing the hour

To show us Your power.

So much power, You have.

The power to make; the power to give;

The power to take...

Truly, we thank You, God, for your name's sake,

And for Your power to awake,

For to glorify You and to make You smile;

And you, oh, Lord, to never beguile.

The Power of the Tongue

May You, Lord, control my tongue
With whomever I'm among.
Let it speak no evil
Nor cause upheaval.
Let it be used for all things good—
And if I speak like You, it would.
Let it speak no lies on no big U's or no little I's;
Let it carry words only of You.
Let it help build lives and make them anew.
Last but not least, here's something to feast:
Whatever you say, let it be true.

The Ultimate Sacrifice

Obedience is free

Cause Jesus hung on the tree,

So we could be free.

When Jesus asked His Father, "Why?"

And He didn't reply,

Never once did Jesus deny.

Imagine what He must have thought:

My father let me hang here to be slought.

He hung there in such agony;

He just let it be.

A tear, he shedded as the nails threaded.

His Father never explained,

But Jesus never complained.

God wanted to show the people who He is,

To give His Son a story,

And to give Him glory;

To write it in the sand,

So His people would have a helping hand;

So their sins would be wiped away

In hopes they would glorify Him one day.

He gave us new life we never had;

He didn't even care that we were bad.

To not read His story,

Recognize Him, and give Him glory,

Makes Him sad.

The Way It Was vs. the Way It Is
(My Testimony)

Even though I knew I was lost,

I'd still would take a hit at any cost.

And in the morning, when I got sane,

I would look around and see no gain—

Nothing but pain.

I was in the street,

Just grooving to the beat;

I had nothing to feed the spirit.

If somebody tried to tell me, I didn't want to hear it.

I did things my way and thought it was okay,

Until one night I went to bed, and I began to dream.

I saw my life so out of control,

And then it started to unfold.

The ground I stood on was hot,

and everything around it.

My soul yearned and burned

As though it was lit;

I knew I needed to make up my mind,

And needed to do it well,

Cause in my dream, my soul had gone to hell.

When I awoke, I cried to the Lord,

"Can I please come to you?

I promise, I give up; if you'll just make me new."

(cont.)

At first, it seemed so hard when I cried to the Lord.
The more I prayed and the more I read,
The more my spirit got fed.
Again, I fell to my knees;
I cried, "Lord, help me, please!"
My mind began to feel at ease.
Somehow I knew the Lord had healed me from this disease.
The Lord opened a new door
On December 17, 2004.

This Light of Mine

Be a light everywhere you go;

Don't you be afraid to let Jesus show.

Let your conversation be His Word,

Maybe someone somewhere never heard.

Let them hear His story and give God the glory;

Hope it pierces their hearts and they become a part,

Then they can let their light shine cause they learned of someone

greater than themselves

To help them change their mind.

Let's hope the Good News

Helps someone else to choose.

This Too Shall Pass

Loneliness crowds the mind with doubt

Cause of all the things we think about.

So many thoughts in our heads

Wreck our sleep when we go to bed.

We think about the things for God we want to do,

And the list we compile is a whole slew.

We think about the living, and we think about the dead,

But then we think about what the Bible said:

"For the wages of sin is death."

Maybe it's just a test.

It all began with a thought:

Think about Jesus, and the good fight He fought;

All the souls he healed;

And how things like loneliness were sealed.

Think about Jesus in that lonely tomb

And how lonely we must have been

In our mother's womb.

Nothing hindered or held us back;

We both came out as a matter of fact.

If for God we live and for God we die,

Then loneliness should just pass by.

Loneliness is just a phase.

Thank God we can look forward to better days!

Tic Toc

We should serve like Jesus;

Do it without a fuss.

Preach like Paul to encourage all.

Have a Noah spirit; be sure someone hears it.

Let your trust be not in man;

Make sure it's in Jesus—He can.

Build your home on solid ground;

Use only material of which Christianity was found.

Stop watching the clock; start depending on the Rock.

Stop looking at the door; try giving it a knock.

Those demons in your life, He'll block.

Count your blessings; call them lessons.

Use everything God has given unto you;

Only then will you live life anew.

To Each His Own
(Testimony)

Maybe while I'm praying, down on my knees,

You're grinding leaves and smoking trees.

Or maybe you're filling your tank

With your favorite drink.

Or maybe you're using drugs

And just need a hug.

But what I remember most,

I gave up the Ghost. You see,

I haven't always been set free; this used to be me.

If you, at the time, God didn't choose,

It doesn't mean He wants you to lose.

He's waiting for you to get tired of your mess;

He's wanting to offer you His best.

Sometimes God wants us to prove

That we're truly finished with our groove.

Sometimes God will give us a test

To see if we're at our best.

And to see if His name,

We Acclaim.

True Love

God will give you life, brand new,

All He asks is that you be true

Here's what you need to perfect:

He's a God of no respect.

If He did it for me,

He'll do it for you.

God is just all about, and never doubt

He loves you more than you'll ever know.

But it's your love for Him, He wants you to show.

When praises go up, blessings come down.

He proves to you, true love, you've found;

God can make your life more abound.

Just knowing this, you should be astounded.

Trust And Never Doubt

Whenever life gets hard,

The Lord and I don't grow apart.

If anything, it makes us close.

I just chop it up as being a dose.

Things go wrong; no matter how strong,

We all have trouble and sometimes double.

But when trouble comes to my door,

It makes me love Him more.

He holds my hand

And walks me through.

If he'll do it for me, He'll do it for you.

If you pack up and turn your back,

The more your life will lack.

When life gets hard, you just keep trusting in the Lord.

Uncertain

Sometimes life can throw a curve ball,
But we are still blessed through it all.
Sometimes life gets hard to bear,
But it's such a joy knowing someone cares.
Sometimes life can be a drag,
But we can't fix it, so why do we brag?
Sometimes life is being caught in the rain,
But it can soothe the soul and heal the pain.
Sometimes life just needs to be told
How we all fall short but still meet our goal.
Sometimes life should be a clue
That God is in control;
We see it with our own eyes
Cause He takes us from young to old.
Sometimes, it seems, too often His story goes untold.
If you want to go to heaven, the way has been paved.
Through faith, you'll need to be saved.

Say "Father, please,
Save my soul;
Clean me up and make me whole
In hopes I'll see you one day.
In Jesus' name, I pray."

(cont.)

Then sometimes life becomes so alive
That we cannot describe.
How complaints become restraints
Because in God, we abide.

Unconditional Love

Jesus will meet you wherever you are;
It doesn't matter, near or far.
He only cares about the troubles you bear;
He's not concerned about what you wear.
Conditions doesn't matter either—
You can come messed up; give it all to Him,
And He'll fill your cup.
It'll be alright in the morning
From whence comes your joy.
He'll supply your needs;
He'll even give you poi.
You can take a simple hope each day
And let Him lead the way.
He'll bless your life in so many ways,
And so many benefits, He pays.
Give no power to man cause he can't,
But Jesus can.

Unspeakable Joy

Thank you, Lord, for so much joy.
Of You, sometimes, I may seem coy.
I'm not just trying to get by or trying to deny;
I want to be sure of what I do or say.
You, I want to please in every way.
When I speak Your Word, I want it to be true;
Lord, help me to speak it just like You.
When I give You praise, I want it to be real,
To show some lost soul, it is You who heals.
Lord, make me bold,
To tell a dying world
You can save their soul.
Lord, teach me to be humble,
To be like you and never mumble.
Help me live my life in all your ways.
Lord, I believe this could add to my days.

Vain

One day your life became a struggle
And you began to juggle.
You try to blame it on the Lord,
But you didn't do your part.
You did those things not pleasing to God,
And that's what makes life hard.
 You robbed Peter to pay Paul,
But you never made the call;
Then you died,
And you lost it all.

Wait

Waiting on the Lord can sometimes seem hard.

Our way gets dark,

Our hearts get heavy,

Our minds get lost,

But we should wait on the Lord

At any cost.

We should pray and pray

Till we hear the Lord say,

"Hold on, my child, it'll be okay."

If we continue to pray day by day,

He'll lead us and guide us His way.

We have nothing to lose,

But a chance to choose to not accept strife

And where we live our next life.

Will it be heaven, or will it be hell?

Wherever it is,

We need to choose it well.

Waymaker

Lord, You gave us another day and started us on our way

With a mind to pray

And a voice to say the things we need

And a Word to heed.

You show us love from heaven above,

And You help us to cope when we have no hope.

Lord, You gave us another day to tell our story and give You glory.

How You made a way!

"What If?" World

What if God told Jesus to tell the Holy Spirit
To tell all your friends,
The world is coming to an end,
Cause He's getting near it?
To tell thy people
 "No more time for all things petty"
And that they better be ready.
To have a made-up mind
Or be left behind.
That, "Unless they heed to what I need,
Here is what they will find."
They'll never be able to tell;
Their souls, they lost to a burning hell
Cause they did not make up their minds in time.

Witness

There ain't no gain in being ashamed
Cause you're living your life in vain.
If you give it to God,
He can make it all change
And so much more that you can attain;
Like peace and joy, and happiness, too.
If He did it for me, He'll do it for you.
He can make your life brand-new.
Now, I can't tell you what to do
Cause it's all up to you.
I'm just a witness who can declare to you, it's true.

World Changers

If the world were a toy
For a little girl or a little boy,
Would they see anything good,
Or would it look like the hood?
Would it show them anything
From those here first,
Or would their little minds continue to thirst?
Would it show them how to get their souls saved?
Would it show how, "the way," we didn't pave?
Would it show them the Bible and that they should read it?
Would it show them anything about life,
Just a little bit?
Would it show them the cross and Jesus Christ?
Would it show them what He did for them
And how He paid the ultimate price?

Worthy to Be Praised

Lord, You're wonderful and worthy to be praised.

We thank You, Lord, for we are so wonderfully made.

Thank You, Lord, for Your breath of life;

Thank You, Lord, for Your sacrifice.

We're sorry, Lord, for when we were lost,

For never remembering who paid the cost.

Lord, You opened up our eyes,

And for that, we're obliged.

We thank You, Lord, for Your supplies

For all our needs, and for our spirits,

You feed.

We come to You with arms opened wide

Cause our junk, we learned, we couldn't hide.

We plead to You, oh, Lord,

That in You we will abide,

If you will just let us in and take away our sin.

Jeremiah 33:3 said, "Call unto me, and I will answer thee,

and show thee great and mighty things, which thoust knowest not."

What are you waiting for? It's not like He's pulling your name from a pot.

Worthy

When I found Jesus, I found a prize.
At the mention of his name, I rise.
At the mention of His Word, I hear
He knew from the start I would need an ear.
At the mention of His works,
I give Him His perks,
For it is in Him where the truth lurks.
At the mention of His promises,
I give Him praise,
A child of His, one day,
He knew He would raise
To help spread the Good News
And help His people choose
Right from wrong.
For He knew this would glorify
His Father on the throne.